HOSPITAL LINGO

HOSPITAL LINGO

A Patient's Guide to Hospital Speak

J. K. Moore

Library of Congress Control Number: 2019913459
ISBN: Hardcover   978-1-7960-5768-3
              Softcover   978-1-7960-5767-6
              eBook   978-1-7960-5766-9

Print information available on the last page.

Rev. date: 09/04/2019

To order additional copies of this book, contact:
Xlibris
1-888-795-4274
www.Xlibris.com
Orders@Xlibris.com
800962

Thank You

Many thanks to all who shared
their expertise and knowledge to make
Hospital Lingo happen.
Hippa

"About your privacy rights ..."

Contents

Intro

One of the things that can be even more frustrating than being hospitalized as a patient is not being able to understand what hospital staff is saying to you or about you. Most people don't realize how confusing Hospital Lingo can be.

For this reason, I offer this humorous guide for patients, their families, and friends.

Hospital Lingo 101

Orientation and Terminology

We hope this book helps you feel better and get well soon. Remember, laughter is the best medicine.

Admitted

Congratulations, you just got Admitted.

Admitted is another good example. In Hospital Lingo, hospital admission is not like being admitted into a movie theater or a concert or an admission or confession like you cracked on the witness stand during a trial or under tough questioning and a hot light at the police station, as in "Yes ... Yes ... It was me! I did it!" In Hospital Lingo, it's not that kind of Admitted.

Being Admitted in Hospital Lingo is far more like getting admitted into college. If you have really positive test results and scores, you may qualify. Much like college admission, for hospital admission, you have to fill out a lot of forms to be Admitted. Factors like a high fever or chest pain are like high SAT scores or ranking at the top of your class. Your chances of admission increase in both cases.

Once you are an Inpatient and are Admitted, anyone who comes to see you who doesn't work at the hospital is called a visitor. Hospitals usually have visiting hours and a specific time that you have to leave when visiting hours are over. This makes being Admitted in Hospital Lingo more like prison than college or the movie theater.

The succeeding is offered to explain that the use of language in hospitals is different. Hospitals use a lot of words or terms or abbreviations that mean something quite different in day-to-day life than they do in the hospital. Once you are Admitted, the new terms will begin popping up in the context of what we call Hospital Lingo.

Patients and Patience

The reason I think they call you the Patient is because you will need to be Patient! There are times when you will have to *wait*! The only people better at making others wait are the airlines. Hospitals require Patients and Patience. If you are not able to exercise Patience, the frustration might get to you before the disease or illness does.

Anticipating the need to wait and be Patient is a good way to manage your own expectations. I often wonder who thought up the term *Patient* and what inspired it. One might speculate the term *Patient* comes from your need to have Patience to deal with the hospital. Once you get into one of those fancy electronic beds with buttons and switches and a remote control in a room with real walls (not curtains), you have just become an Inpatient. However, as next discussed, there are different types of Patients, i.e., Inpatients, Outpatients, and Observation Patients, etc. All Patients require Patience.

Patient

Inpatients and Outpatients

Not every Patient gets Admitted. There are generally two primary or typical flavors of Patients, Inpatients and Outpatients. Inpatients are expected to stay overnight and are generally Admitted as discussed. Outpatients go home the same day. In Hospital Lingo, if you are an Outpatient, your hospital encounter is typically called a visit. Only Inpatients are Admitted. To make it extra confusing, you can get stuck between the Inpatient and Outpatient universes and become what Hospital Lingo calls an Observation Patient. That means the hospital might keep you overnight as an Inpatient or let you go home as an Observation Patient. They aren't quite sure whether the hospital will keep you overnight or not—yet.

Positive and Negative

Typically, anything in life defined as Positive is good, and anything described as Negative is not good. In Hospital Lingo, it is just the opposite—Positive is not good, and Negative is good—when you get your test results. You want your test results to come back Negative. That's a good thing! If your test results are Positive, that is not a good thing.

A doctor or nurse who informs you of Positive results will usually be frowning and look concerned. It may mean you have been diagnosed, and the hospital knows what is wrong. Next, you can expect the hospital is probably going to run more tests, one to confirm the first results and then further tests to assure they are on the right track toward an accurate diagnosis. Positive results often mean that you are probably not leaving soon or you may need to make a return visit.

Hospital Lingo

Humorous vs. Humerus

For something to be Humorous, it should make you laugh, right?

In Hospital Lingo, there is nothing funny about it. If you are headed to the hospital or are already there, know that it is a bone—and not the funny bone, but close to it.

Well, in Hospital Lingo, the Humerus is actually the name of the bone that goes from your shoulder to your elbow. If someone says your Humerus is fractured, it doesn't mean your sense of humor is broken. It's your arm.

Humorous vs. Humerus

"Humerus fractures!"
"Well, Doc, I don't see what's so funny."

Bypass

In Hospital Lingo, a Bypass is not the interstate highway you must take to get around inner-city traffic. Rather, in Hospital Lingo, a Bypass is a relatively serious surgery using blood vessels from one part of your body to replace vessels that may be blocked around your heart (see "Cabbage or CABG").

Cabbage or CABG

A CABG is neither a green vegetable used to make coleslaw nor something often served as a side with corned beef. In Hospital Lingo, CABG stands for coronary artery bypass graft.

A CABG is a pretty serious surgical procedure where the surgeon removes blood vessels, typically veins, from one part of the Patient and uses them to replace arteries around the heart that are blocked.

CABGs have become successful in frequent surgeries to fix heart-related chest pain. However, they are being offset now by something called a stent. Stents are later discussed.

Cabbage or CABG

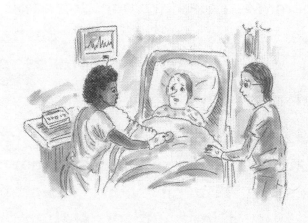

"We think you'll need a CABG."
"It's my least favorite veggie."

ICU

Unfortunately, in Hospital Lingo, ICU is not the most common adult response while playing peek-a-boo with babies. In Hospital Lingo, "I see you" doesn't mean you've been spotted.

It also doesn't mean putting you on ice or that you are an icy person.

It is a place called the intensive care unit. There are a few different flavors of ICUs, like CICU (cardiac intensive care unit) and NICU (neonatal intensive care unit) for premature babies.

ICU

Port

In Hospital Lingo, a Port is not the next place the cruise ship will pull into the harbor or an indiscriminate safe place in a storm or a sweet, fortified Portuguese wine served by rich people after dinner.

In Hospital Lingo, a Port usually looks like a hard plastic straw or tube that is typically inserted beneath the skin to deliver medication, to use as a catheter, or to draw blood. Ports are generally a good thing and help get stuff in and out of the Patient without going through the painful process of an insertion each time.

Port

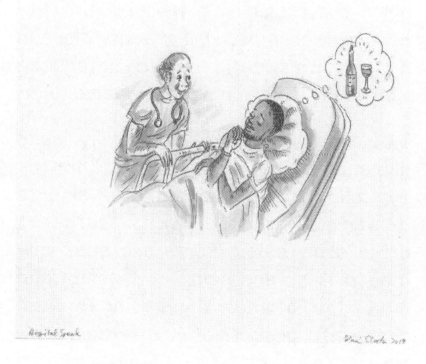

"We are going to give you a port!"
"Ah ... a glass of Madeira would be nice."

Void

Most people think of a Void as a large, dark empty space or a word you write on a cancelled check. In Hospital Lingo, *Void* is not a noun and does not mean an empty space or a word you write on a check you started but screwed up and couldn't use. Void in Hospital Lingo is what we call urination—or in lay terms, a number 1 or a tinkle (also a pee-pee or a whiz or powdering one's nose). *Void* generally comes up when somebody, like a nurse, tells you that you need to Void before you can leave.

Before I learned Hospital Lingo, I always thought that *Void* was a noun. Much like the word *ditch* in air travel, the noun *Void* becomes a verb—to Void (an act)— in Hospital Lingo.

Do not worry when the hospital says you have to Void before you can leave. The hospital is just checking to make sure all your systems are working properly before you say goodbye.

Void

Stat

Stat in Hospital Lingo has nothing to do with points or rebounds per game or Stat scores or a collection of numbers. In Hospital Lingo, *Stat* means "right away," "hurry up," "immediately," "quickly," or "ASAP"—as in lickety-split or Johnny on the spot or step it up right now!

SOB

First and foremost, this is not the word *sob*, meaning "crying softly but aloud." *SOB* is an abbreviation in Hospital Lingo like in day-to-day life. In Hospital Lingo, the abbreviation *SOB* means "shortness of breath"—not the male offspring of a dog or a person you do not like who is behaving badly.

If you happen to see *SOB* written in your medical chart or record, don't jump to the wrong conclusion. It means "short of breath." For example, if you read "Ms. Jones in 3202 is SOB," it generally means "short of breath" or "shortness of breath."

Now this isn't to say there won't be some hospital staff you don't like or who doesn't like you. You might hear some hospital staff use this term in the regular sense (hopefully outside of earshot), or you might hear it if some hospital staff accidentally drops something heavy on their foot or the hospital computer system goes down. At which point, you *can* assume they are using the regular SOB.

SOB

"That lady is short of breath."

IV

In Hospital Lingo, an IV is not like poison ivy—that itchy weed or the girlfriend of Selena in Batman. It is also not the leafy green stuff that grows on the buildings of the campuses of overpriced but highly ranked colleges in the northeast United States. Rather, in Hospital Lingo, IV means "intravenous." An IV usually refers to a plastic fluid-filled bag or bags with a small hose-like tubing and a needle at the end to put fluids into your body.

IVs come in many flavors. These fluid-filled bags usually say stuff like "Dextrose" or "Saline" with numbers and barcoding stamped on the outside. The neat thing about IVs is that some come hanging from a long upright pole on a base with wheels attached, notably called an IV pole.

Be careful getting on and off elevators with them. This IV rolling pole thingy allows the Patient to get around the hospital with the IV still attached.

IV

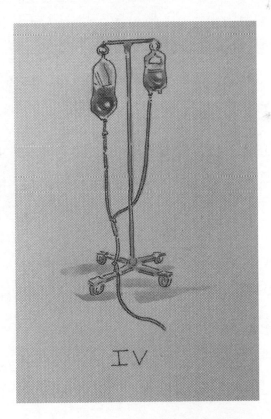

IV

Eloped

In Hospital Lingo, *Eloped* doesn't mean two people who ran off and got married without telling anybody. In Hospital Lingo, Eloped means that you escaped.

It means the hospital doesn't know where you are and when you left. It also generally means the hospital staff wasn't expecting you to leave and doesn't know exactly how or why you left.

The hospital typically treats elopement the way the police treat a missing-persons case. They start by interrogating potential witnesses, including staff and neighboring Patients, when they might have last seen you and what you were wearing.

One of the reasons I think hospitals use backless gowns is to prevent people from eloping, or escaping. Any person with sufficient dignity to worry about exposing their backside or who can't run backward might have difficulty getting away.

So in Hospital Lingo, *Eloped*, unlike marriage, definitively means "escaped" (not "got divorced"—hint, hint!). And *AMA* (more on this later) the first thing the hospital writes down in your medical chart if they can't figure how or when you got away.

Eloped

"I'm concerned the patient will elope."
"Not a chance! We aren't
even engaged."

Arrest

In Hospital Lingo, *Arrest* does not mean "taken into custody by law enforcement." In Hospital Lingo, *Arrest* typically comes in two flavors: respiratory Arrest and cardiac Arrest. Neither flavor is good. But on the bright side, if you hear the term in a hospital, it generally means you made it.

Although there is never anything good about the terms *Arrest* or *Arrested* when they apply to you, the good news is that the best place for an Arrest to occur is in the hospital. Almost all hospitals have a rapid response team skilled at making sure any type of hospital Arrest is managed quickly by medical experts.

Arrest is often stated in the past tense, i.e. *Arrested*. That's because the hospital makes sure most Patients come through it okay. (See "Clear" and "Code and Coded" for greater clarification.)

Defib

Defib isn't a description of a lie told by an illiterate person but the abbreviation for *defibrillator*.

Defibrillators deliver a dose of electric current, often called a countershock, to the heart (see "Clear" and "Code and Coded").

Escort Service

In Hospital Lingo, calling the Escort Service will not result in a woman in high heels coming to your room to get to know you better for a price. Nor will it result in a truck with flashing lights on top with two rednecks inside coming to drive in front of your vehicle while you pull your trailer down a two-lane road. In Hospital Lingo, the Escort Service is a bunch of relatively strong and physically fit hospital staff members who push Patients in wheelchairs or on gurneys around the hospital or out the door when discharged. They usually have a great sense of humor and several interesting stories to tell.

Escort Service

"Your escort service is here!"
"Hmmm ... not quite what I expected!"

Coverage

Coverage in Hospital Lingo does not refer to a news reporter or newspaper with a story that makes the final edition of the evening news. It has nothing to do with liability or collision or a description of the defense against a pass in a football game.

It is also not someone's explanation provided to a spouse or significant other explaining why they got home so late last night.

Rather, in Hospital Lingo, it's more like auto coverage, but far more complex. If asked about Coverage in Hospital Lingo, this pertains to your health insurance and how much you pay as the Patient verses your health insurance.

Insure vs. Ensure

Any time a Patient hears the word Insure related to a hospital stay, most believe the hospital is talking about money, health insurance, and payment for hospital services.

Although that may be true in the business side of the hospital, on the clinical side, *Insure* is really spelled with an e, *Ensure* and typically refers to a product used and a method of tube feeding to the Patient in receiving proper nutrition.

Ensure is actually the brand or trade name for nutritional supplements or meal replacements made by Abbott Laboratories.

Much like the term *Xerox* has come to mean "copy" or like *Kleenex* means "tissue," Ensure in Hospital Lingo typically refers to a liquid food supplement fed to Patients through a tube.

CAT

In Hospital Lingo, a CAT has nothing to do with a furry pet with claws and an attitude that prances around the house doing whatever it wishes.

In Hospital Lingo, CAT is an acronym for computerized axial tomography.

This is a fancy kind of X-ray that allows the hospital to take very rapid and very finely sliced X-rays to put together a three-dimensional picture of whatever the hospital is trying to look at inside of you. It is *not* the kind of cat that meows, has whiskers and claws, and is a member of the feline family.

CAT

"This is the CAT scan machine."
"How do you get the cat to
stay in that thing?!"

Stool

A Stool is not a four-legged chair without a back that you sit on at a bar. In Hospital Lingo, a Stool is what we refer to as a number 2.

It has always surprised me how much can be learned from the frequency or observation or examination of a Stool in hospitals.

Acuity

Acuity is not a word used by a chauvinist male Patient to describe the petite, new, attractive female nurse on the evening shift. It also has nothing to do with how smart or intelligent you are or are not, like your IQ.

In Hospital Lingo, *Acuity* means "severity." Your Acuity level is the Hospital Lingo measure of how sick you are. The higher your Acuity level, the worse off you are.

You want to flunk the Acuity level test at all costs, if possible, with the lowest possible score.

Be careful to ask for an interpretation of your Acuity from your nurse. In some hospitals, a higher Acuity has a lower number and a lower Acuity has a higher number.

Resident

In Hospital Lingo, the Resident is not the person who lives at your address and constantly gets mail in which you are not interested. Rather, in Hospital Lingo, the Resident is typically a young doctor who has finished medical school but hasn't finished practical hands-on training.

The Residents come in several ranking years: first-year Resident, second-year Resident, etc.

Interestingly enough, although Residents can be male or female, some of them end their Residency by turning into fellows. Isn't that interesting?

Resident

"Meet our new resident!"
"Poor you! You have to live here?!"

BID

BID is not the last dollar amount offered during an auction, but rather, it means two times a day, hence "bi."

TID

TID is not to be confused with TID— time in detention. It means "three times daily," or "tri."

QID

QID is not a form of British currency. In Hospital Lingo, *QID* means "four times a day," or "quarterly."

PRN

As if things weren't already confusing enough, more new Hospital Lingo was needed for things that weren't going to happen once, twice, or three times a day.

So Hospital Lingo invented another imperceptible acronym: PRN. *PRN* means "whenever necessary" or "as needed" or even "right now," if it seems like a good time.

Hospital Lingo

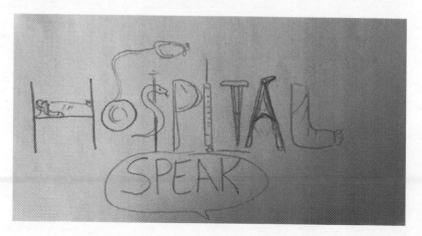

Stent

Stent is a noun and not a verb in Hospital Lingo. So if you're thinking, "My brother or nephew in the marines did a three-month stint, or tour, in Afghanistan," you are thinking of the wrong stint.

In Hospital Lingo, a Stent is a tiny, tiny metal tube that is collapsed and threaded through a blood vessel to a blockage and then popped open so blood can flow. It is a pretty nifty innovation in treating heart problems and probably preferred to CABG if given the choice.

Rest

When in the hospital and sedation is considered, there are several stages of Rest used to describe the result of sedation in Hospital Lingo.

Restless generally means "needs more sedation."
Restful means "sufficient sedation."
Finally, *Resting* is "too much sedation."

Restraint

In day-to-day life, Restraint can be described as not telling a friend their new haircut doesn't look very good or figuratively biting your tongue when someone says something dumb or stupid or false in your presence.

In Hospital Lingo, Restraint can be physical or pharmaceutical, but it is a means of tying a hospital Patient down to their bed or using enough of a sedative so you are sure the Patient isn't going anywhere. Restraints in Hospital Lingo are most often applied when a Patient represents a risk of physical harm to themselves, hospital staff, or other Patients. It means the doctor has decided you are at risk of harming yourself or others, and due to this, you require sedation or physical Restraints.

Clear

Clear may be one of the last words you ever want to hear in Hospital Lingo. This is especially true if the person saying it is yelling it really loudly. *Clear* is not a word you want to hear exclaimed aloud even as a bystander.

In Hospital Lingo, *Clear* is not associated with the weather or used in a colloquialism—like the coast is clear or water, chicken broth, Jell-O, or ginger ale as a clear liquid diet. *Clear* does not refer to a good explanation to a complex concept once explained.

Clear is most often shouted loudly during a Code, as defined herein, when a Patient has an Arrest, also defined herein.

Usually, there is a hospital person standing over a prone Patient rubbing two miniature paddles together. This is quickly followed by a feeling described by the clearees, or Patient survivors, as being hit by a tractor trailer.

Code or Coded

In Hospital Lingo, a Code has nothing to do with software, like the stuff that runs your laptop computer. It also has nothing to do with valor and honesty, like a code of conduct or a coded or secret message used during World War II to transmit secret messages. Rather, in the Hospital Lingo, *Code* can be a noun or a verb, a.k.a. "calling a Code" versus "the Patient Coded."

If you have Coded or a Code is called, it means your clinical condition rapidly declined to a point where important body functions, like your heartbeat or breathing, have stopped. If you Code, you may be in need of resuscitation where a Code team is called for rapid response. If you experience a Code, see "Clear" or "Arrest" for greater clarification as to what happens.

Discharge

Discharge doesn't mean you left the military honorably or dishonorably.

Discharge in Hospital Lingo has one of two meanings. The first is that you're going home, and the second, well, I'm not sure you really want to know, but see "Specimen."

DVT

In Hospital Lingo, *DVT* is not a reference to the flat screen on the wall in your hospital room. You were not listening carefully enough. It's not "dee TV."

Some Patients actually thought this was a satellite dish or cable service or a shiny, flat disk one puts into a DVD player to watch a movie.

It really stands for deep vein thrombosis. DVTs are clots in the veins affecting blood flow. It's not good, but it is a manageable medical condition.

DVT

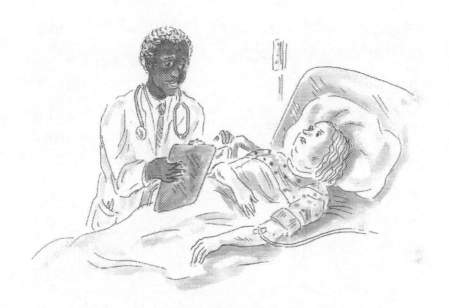

"I put in an order for a DVT."
"The last thing I want to do is
watch a movie right now, Doctor."

Incontinent

Incontinent is not to be confused with intercontinental travel within the USA except Hawaii. Rather, in Hospital Lingo, it generally means the unanticipated appearance of urine in your bed or clothes. It also means you Voided (see "Void") unexpectedly. There are many solutions once this problem is known, and it is not uncommon. Don't be embarrassed. The hospital sees and successfully treats many Patients who become Incontinent.

Incontinence

Incontinence is not the plural or verbal version of *Incontinent*. If being Incontinent occurs on repeated occasions, the letters *ce* replace the ending letter *t*. I was all for calling it bladder recidivism—a repeat offender sort of thing, but that sounded way to legal!

Hospital Lingo

Litter

In Hospital Lingo, Litter isn't trash on the side of the road or a group of beautiful young kittens.

In Hospital Lingo, a Litter is like a stretcher, sometimes with wheels. Now to make things even more confusing, hospitals also have these things called gurneys.

Contrary to popular belief, a gurney is not a dairy cow from New Jersey. A gurney is a Litter, or stretcher, with wheels.

Litter

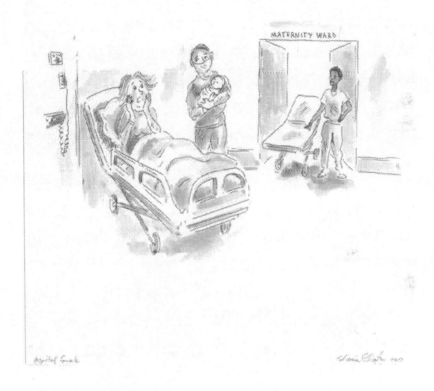

"Your litter has arrived."
"You mean I had more than one?"

AMA

Before I learned Hospital Lingo, I thought *AMA* referred to the American Medical Association, and it still does. But *AMA* in Hospital Lingo doesn't stand for the venerable professional group of physicians and other medical providers with nice offices in Chicago.

Rather, in Hospital Lingo, it actually means "against medical advice." It literally means that the hospital told the Patient that they needed to do something, like not leave, and the Patient—that's you—refused to accept that advice and left anyway.

AMA comes up most often in Hospital Lingo when a Patient decides to leave the emergency department even though the hospital staff had told them not do so.

If AMA happens, it usually involves filling out a lot of forms and the hospital staff using their best persuasive efforts to keep you from leaving. For the most notable AMA situations, go back and reference "Eloped." When a Patient leaves and no one in the hospital knows when they left or where they went, somebody on the hospital staff starts charting AMA as soon as possible.

It looks bad enough if a Patient splits and nobody notices or knows until they are already gone. It's far worse if the chart or medical record does not reflect that the Patient left against medical advice or the Patient did something or refused to do something the hospital told the Patient to do or not to do.

It's also typically the best explanation the hospital can offer if you Elope and something goes wrong later. AMA is a Hospital Lingo version of "I told you so," and it will likely be written in the Patient's medical record and history.

AOB

In Hospital Lingo, *AOB* means "alcohol on breath." Unlike the incredibly solemn and custodial reaction of the state highway patrol, the hospital will use this lingo to convey to other hospital staff that something more than your medical problem might be in play.

It could affect the extent of which your account of symptoms is believable or accurate or could be a reason, especially if you are in the emergency department after a car accident, to be an observation that lawyers might call a contributing factor. Regardless, AOB is better served as a medical observation or diagnosis in Hospital Lingo than a citation by law enforcement.

Stroke

You've probably already got this one, but to be certain, *Stroke* is not a word being yelled through a megaphone at the crew team at Harvard and not Serena Williams's excellent form when serving or hitting a tennis ball or the act used to describe petting a purring kitten in your lap.

Rather, it means some blood vessel in the brain got clogged up and caused you to go to the hospital. Even if you are in the hospital for this one, there is a lot the hospital can do to help.

Labor

In Hospital Lingo, *Labor* is not the day marking the unofficial end of summer or the people on the staff who work there. In Hospital Lingo, it means the baby is on the way. Active Labor is like hearing final approach when flying. Strap yourself in! There is a mom on the runway in Labor, preparing for a delivery.

Labor can also be used to refer to breathing which is difficult. "Labored breathing" may appear in your chart even if you are not expecting to have a baby soon.

Birthing

Birthing is a Hospital Lingo developed for marketing purposes. Nobody seemed anxious to go to a place called Labor and Delivery, so the Birthing center or unit was born (pun intended).

Most people seldom ate or ordered squid until they changed the name to calamari, and the Patagonian toothfish is now facing extinction because they changed its name to Chilean sea bass. *Voila!* Now people can't eat enough calamari or Chilean sea bass. Don't worry about the calamari. There are plenty left. I wish I could say the same for the Chilean sea bass.

So in Hospital Lingo, we replaced Labor and Delivery with Birthing center. Now Birthing centers have truly taken off.

Delivery

Delivery in Hospital Lingo has nothing to do with UPS, FedEx, Postal Service, or a pizza. In a pizza delivery, they bring the pizza to you. In Hospital Lingo, *Delivery* means you go to them—them being the hospital. In Hospital Lingo, *Delivery* is, again, both a verb and a noun.

The verb version typically involves a package, but this one has a baby in it. Delivery comes in three flavors: special (like a breeched birth), vaginal, or a C-section Delivery.

The noun version is usually followed by the word *suite*, not sweet. The Delivery suite is the place where the hospital takes the mom for the event known as the Delivery.

Afterbirth

Afterbirth in Hospital Lingo is a noun, and it's a doozy. It does not mean some time subsequent to birth.

During the Delivery of our first child, while sweating, trembling, and standing in a corner wearing a face mask and a floppy paper hat, I thought we were having twins and the second one didn't look so good. Until someone told me *that* was the placenta, or Afterbirth. Ahem! Live and learn.

Acquired

Acquired in Hospital Lingo means pretty much the same as it does in normal life. But instead of acquiring a new car, in the hospital, this may mean you got an infection from someone or something after you came into the hospital.

Hospital Acquired, or nosocomial, infections get a lot of press about this problem nowadays. Hospitals are working hard to decrease this risk.

NPO

NPO is not Vietnamese takeout food. In Hospital Lingo, *NPO* means "nothing by mouth." This does not mean no food and nutrition cannot be provided to you by some other means. Don't let your imagination wander too much on this one. 'Nuff said.

Just no food by mouth.

Oh, by the way, *PO* in Hospital Lingo means "can be served by mouth," not an absence of wealth or an expression of sadness as in "Po' Ms. Simpson had to go to the hospital today."

Advanced

Advanced is a word that is seldom used to describe you. In Hospital Lingo, *Advanced* usually means the disease or condition that got you Admitted to the hospital is moving ahead. Unlike the board game Monopoly, *Advanced* is not a good word in the Hospital Lingo. No Patient ever Advanced to going home (see "Discharge").

MOM

MOM does not mean the loving female who bore, raised, and cared for you. In Hospital Lingo, if you see this acronym in your Patient medical record, it means "milk of magnesia."

Despite the distinction in Hospital Lingo and day-to-day life, MOM is still living up to her, or its, reputation of being thorough yet gentle.

MOM

M.O.M.

Ula

In Hospital Lingo, *Ula* is typically a suffix or ending to a word. Words like *fistula*, *cannula*, or *fibula* in Hospital Lingo are nothing like regular day-to-day use of the suffix. Examples of common use of the suffix includes *spatula*, *nebula*, *boolah-boolah*, etc. In Hospital Lingo, any word ending in *Ula* is generally a description of a disease or a hospital device that may not be fun.

Guarded

This doesn't generally mean there is a guy with a firearm outside your hospital door, although that does sometimes happen in the hospital. In Hospital Lingo, Guarded refers to your condition clinically and otherwise.

Guarded also means you might make it, but the hospital isn't certain of your condition, unlike Stable, which means you're not getting worse. Guarded means they are watching you closely, and the hospital doesn't wish to be wrong or lose you.

Abscess

Abscess in Hospital Lingo should not be confused with *obsess*, even though they sound alike. *Obsess* refers to binge watching or waiting outside overnight to be among the first to purchase the next iPhone.

An Abscess, in Hospital Lingo, is a space inside of or on your body that should not be there and may have collected or is filled with some stuff that also should not be there. It is most often caused by an infection or the decomposition of tissue.

But typically, the hospital can fix it.

Abscessed

"Baseball injury? I see ...
You're abscessed."

"Not really. I don't even
want to play anymore."

Aggressive

Aggressive is not the term used to describe people who are pushy or trying to move a relationship along faster than the other person would like.

It also does not refer to hospital staff who raise their voices when instructing Patients who are not hard of hearing or seem to be insistent on your course of care.

Typically, in Hospital Lingo, *Aggressive* is used as a description of a disease or condition that is advancing more rapidly than anticipated.

Afebrile

Afebrile simply means you don't have a fever, but it sounds very chic and professional. Hospital staff using this term could simply have said "No fever," but sounding professional is an important part of the hospital staff mystique. Being Afebrile is very, very good.

VENT

Two clues: It is definitely not that thing with slats on the ceiling or in the wall where air comes blowing out. It also doesn't describe the loud and visceral verbal convenience of an emotional expression of disappointment from one person to another, like I had to get that off my chest.

In Hospital Lingo, *Vent* is a shortened term for *ventilator*. A Vent is a machine used to facilitate breathing when Patients cannot breathe on their own. The Vent is commonly used in the hospital's intensive care unit (ICU) but can be used in many other places in the hospital.

Once again, this noun can become a verb if you are Vented. The use of a Vent requires the insertion of a breathing tube down the throat of a Patient while the ventilator assists with breathing.

Specimen

Sorry girls, but in this case, a Specimen does not refer to the handsome gentleman in Speedos with well-defined muscles who danced at your girlfriend's bachelorette party last year. In Hospital Lingo, a Specimen is something that used to be a part of you or your body that the hospital took. Most Specimens get sent to the hospital lab.

Just know that anything called a Specimen used to be part of you—the hospital has it now, and the hospital doesn't know exactly what it is yet either. Also, note that unlike spare parts removed from a car when repaired, which you can generally have returned to you, the hospital gets to keep the Specimen when you leave.

Tissue

In day-to-day life, a tissue is Kleenex or Puffs or a soft rectangular paper used to blow one's nose. In Hospital Lingo, a Tissue is generally part of a Patient's skin or muscle that may be taken for further evaluation in the hospital laboratory (see "Specimen").

"We need a tissue sample."

Cath or Kath

In Hospital Lingo, *Cath* is not short for Kathy, Catherine, or Kathleen. Hospitals don't used Kath with a *K*, only with a *C*. In Hospital Lingo, *Cath* is short for *catheter*—a tiny, tiny tube or wire that can be inserted into you or your blood vessels to look for stuff, administer stuff, and remove stuff that should not be there.

Again, in Hospital Lingo, *Cath* is both a noun and a verb. A Cath is a procedure; a catheter is the tiny tube used to perform a catheterization. If you hit the jackpot and go to the hospital Cath lab, a doctor will use a catheter to perform a Cath to look into your heart or brain via a blood vessel using a catheter.

It's a really cool technology, and it helps a lot of people. However, there are many flavors of Caths, or catheters, used for many different reasons. Some catheters are inserted into the bladder so the Patient can pee or have a number 1 (see "Void"). In this context, Caths really helps eliminate the need for sufficiently ill Patients to get out of bed to go to the bathroom so often. Caths in all forms help Patients and hospital staff. It is generally not always pleasant but is a good thing for everyone.

Stable

In Hospital Lingo, Stable is not the place we keep the horses. Stable means that although you are not out of the woods yet, the hospital has decided you are not getting worse and you are going make it through your hospitalization okay.

You may hear variations on this term, like the word *Stabilized*. That generally means that you were probably not Stable when you got to the hospital but are now.

Cuffed

Whenever hospital staff tells you they are going to Cuff you, they are not going to place physical restraints around your wrists to take you off to jail, even if you have outstanding traffic violations you didn't pay. In Hospital Lingo, when you get Cuffed, the hospital staff are generally only taking your blood pressure and pulse rate.

I think grandfathers used this term to describe smacking disobedient sons or grandsons upside the head.

The Cuff

Hospital Scenic

"I'm sorry, we have to cuff you."

Terminal

In Hospital Lingo, Terminal is not a big building used to catch trains or airplanes with long security lines or a place to check baggage. It also isn't the movie where Tom Hanks lived for many days at the airport. But please know, in Hospital Lingo, it isn't anywhere near the stop we want the Patient to make.

There are kinder and gentler places for that called hospices. As long as you are in the hospital, it is because they still hope and are trying to make sure you are not Terminal. Typically, Terminal is not a good prognosis, but there are great places called hospices that are designed to assure you arrive there with minimal discomfort and maximum attention to things that will improve your quality of life through management of care.

Terminal anticipates you are nearing your final destination.

For many, if not most, Patients, *Terminal* is a Hospital Lingo indicating to that they are on their way to a better place. We hospital people really believe a better place is a valid, true, and reasonably recurrent destination many of our beloved Patients go when they leave Terminal.

Circling the Drain

Circling the Drain is Hospital Lingo for "not likely to make it" (see "Terminal") or unstable or that you are a potential candidate for a celestial transfer. You won't see this written down anywhere, but you might overhear it. Hopefully they are not talking about you.

Nursing

Most Patients get this one. It doesn't mean a mother is breastfeeding her baby. Once again, a verb in normal conversation, *Nursing* becomes a noun in Hospital Lingo.

Nursing is like the army. It is the largest, most long-standing, and well-established branch of the hospitals' clinical workforce.

Nursing has a lock on the best and most current information of the care needs of Patients in the hospital. Nursing also has an actionable and symbiotic relationship with almost every other part of the hospital. Before my career concluded, I came to believe that Nursing must have both clairvoyance in predicting future hospital events and an intelligence service better than our own CIA. Never make the mistake of predicting what Nursing can or cannot do. Nursing puts up with a lot, but they know a lot, and there is no way the hospital could run without Nursing.

A Final Note

The purpose of this little book is threefold.

First, to familiarize the reader with some, but not all, of the frequent acronyms, synonyms, and abbreviated terms in hospitals that are typically used in day-to-day life.

Second, to make the reader, family members, and friends of the hospital patient laugh.

Last, to use that laughter as medicine to help cure or sustain you, a friend, or a loved one during a visit to the hospital.

Wishing you good health and the best of luck.

Printed in the United States
By Bookmasters